Picture the Past

Life on the Lower East Side

Jennifer Blizin Gillis

Heinemann Library
Chicago, Illinois

© 2003 Heinemann Library
a division of Reed Elsevier Inc.
Chicago, Illinois
Customer Service 888-454-2279
Visit our website at www.heinemannlibrary.com

Produced for Heinemann Library by
    Bender Richardson White.
Editor: Lionel Bender
Designer and Media Conversion: Ben White
Picture Researcher: Cathy Stastny
Production Controller: Kim Richardson

12 11 10 09 08
10 9 8 7 6 5 4 3

Printed and bound by Lake Book Manufacturing, Inc.

Library of Congress Cataloging-in-Publication Data.
Gillis, Jennifer Blizin, 1950-
  Life on the Lower East Side / Jennifer Blizin Gillis.
     p. cm. -- (Picture the past)
Summary: An overview of everyday life in New York City's Lower East Sidefrom 1870 to 1913, focusing on the communities formed by people who shared a common language, religion, and/or cultural traditions.
Includes bibliographical references (p.) and index.
  ISBN 1-4034-3796-9 (1-4034-3796-3) (HC)
  ISBN 1-4034-4287-1 (1-4034-4287-8) (Pbk)
  1. Lower East Side (New York, N.Y.)--Social life and customs--19th century--Juvenile literature. 2. Lower East Side (New York, N.Y.)--Social life and customs--20th century--Juvenile literature. 3. Lower East Side (New York, N.Y.)--Social conditions--Juvenile literature. 4. New York (N.Y.)--Social life and customs--19th century--Juvenile literature. 5. New York (N.Y.)--Social life and customs--20th century--Juvenile literature. 6. New York (N.Y.)--Social conditions--Juvenile literature. (1. New York (N.Y.)--Social life and customs--19th century. 2. New York (N.Y.)--Social life and customs--20th century. 3. New York (N.Y.)--Social conditions. 4. New York (N.Y.)--History--19th century. 5. New York (N.Y.)--History--20th century.) I. Title. II. Series.
  F128.68.L6G55 2003
  974.7'1'008621--dc21
                                    2003005419

Special thanks to Angela McHaney Brown at Heinemann Library for editorial and design guidance and direction.

Acknowledgments
The producers and publishers are grateful to the following for permission to reproduce copyright material:
Corbis Images: cover and pp. 12, 13, 19, 23; Bettmann Archives, pp. 7, 8, 11, 16, 21, 22, 26, 27, 28, 29; Michael S. Yamashita, p. 30; Photo Collection Alexander Alland, Sr., pp. 1, 10, 12. North Wind Pictures, pp. 3, 6, 14, 15, 18, 20. The Bridgeman Art Library/The New-York Historical Society, New York, U.S.A., p. 17.
Illustrations: James Field, p. 9; John James, pp. 4, 25.
Map by Stefan Chabluk.

ABOUT THIS BOOK

This book tells about life on the Lower East Side of New York City from 1870 to 1913. People had been coming to New York City from other countries since the 1600s. But in the middle of the 1800s, millions of people from Italy and Eastern Europe came to the city to live and set up businesses. Most of them were Jewish. People who came from other countries wanted to be near people like themselves. On the Lower East Side, they found other people who spoke the same language, worshiped in the same way, and ate familiar foods.

We have illustrated the book with photographs of people and places in New York City from this time period. We have also included artists' ideas of how people lived in the late 1800s and early 1900s.

The Author

Jennifer Blizin Gillis is an editor and author of nonfiction books and poetry for children. She graduated with a B.A. from Guilford College with a degree in French Literature and Art History. She has taught foreign language and social studies at middle schools in North Carolina, Virginia, and Illinois.

Note to the Reader

Some words are shown in bold, **like this.** You can find out what they mean by looking in the glossary.

CONTENTS

The Lower East Side

Most **immigrants** arriving in New York City started out on the Lower East Side. This neighborhood was near the port of New York, and newcomers could afford to live there. As one group of people moved in, another moved out. At first, it was an Irish neighborhood. Then, it was taken over by immigrants from Germany. As the Lower East Side became a clothes-making center, people from Italy and **Eastern Europe** came to find jobs. By the end of the 1800s, more than 500,000 people lived on the Lower East Side.

Look for these
The illustration of a Lower East Side boy and girl shows you the subject of each two-page story in the book.

The illustration of a man with a **pushcart** marks boxes with interesting facts and figures about life on New York City's Lower East Side.

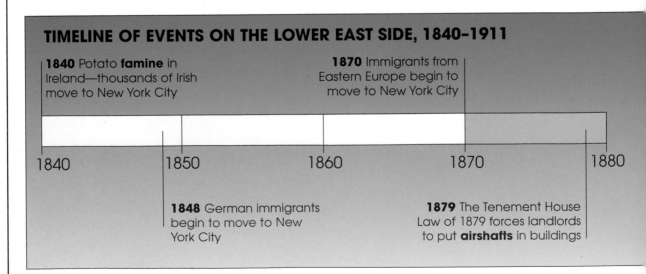

TIMELINE OF EVENTS ON THE LOWER EAST SIDE, 1840–1911

1840 Potato **famine** in Ireland—thousands of Irish move to New York City

1870 Immigrants from Eastern Europe begin to move to New York City

| 1840 | 1850 | 1860 | 1870 | 1880 |

1848 German immigrants begin to move to New York City

1879 The Tenement House Law of 1879 forces landlords to put **airshafts** in buildings

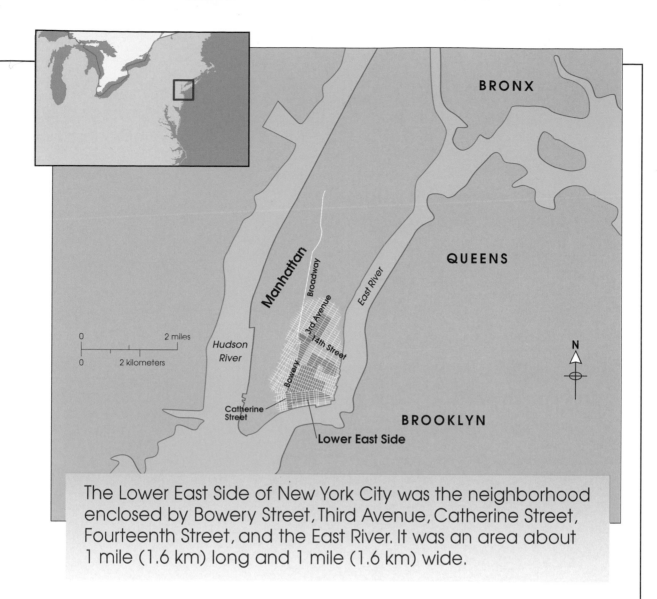

BRONX

QUEENS

Manhattan

Broadway

3rd Avenue

14th Street

East River

Hudson River

Bowery

0   2 miles

0   2 kilometers

Catherine Street

BROOKLYN

Lower East Side

N

The Lower East Side of New York City was the neighborhood enclosed by Bowery Street, Third Avenue, Catherine Street, Fourteenth Street, and the East River. It was an area about 1 mile (1.6 km) long and 1 mile (1.6 km) wide.

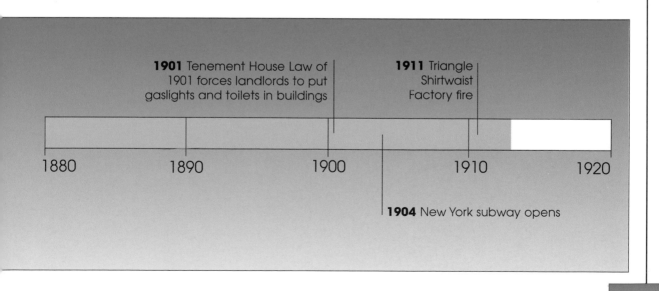

1901 Tenement House Law of 1901 forces landlords to put gaslights and toilets in buildings

1911 Triangle Shirtwaist Factory fire

1880   1890   1900   1910   1920

1904 New York subway opens

A Better World

No matter where they came from,
immigrants thought of the country
they were born in as "the old country."
At first, many of the Italians who
came to New York City were **tailors.**
In the old country, tailors did not
make much money. They thought they
could earn a lot of money in America.
They hoped they could go back to
Italy with the money they earned.

When immigrants
saw the Statue of
Liberty, they knew
they had reached
New York.

The Jewish people who first came from **Eastern Europe** were tailors, too. Life there was difficult for Jewish people. Laws forced them to live only in certain places. They could not own land and were not allowed to have certain jobs. Soldiers attacked Jewish villages. They destroyed homes, shops, and **synagogues.** Eastern Europeans came to the United States to start new homes, jobs, and businesses.

Doctors checked all immigrants—like this mother and her children from Italy— who were brought to Ellis Island. A sick person might be sent back to his or her country. Small boats took immigrants from the island to the city.

Homes

The only homes that **immigrants** could afford were in **tenements.** Tenements were buildings with tiny, dark apartments. There were few windows to let in fresh air. Hallways were especially dark and smelled like garbage. Early apartments had no electricity. Fires from coal stoves, gaslight, and candles were a constant danger. Several family members, and sometimes **boarders,** lived in a one- or two-bedroom apartment. Immigrants often lived and worked in their crowded apartments.

BUILDING LAWS

In 1879, a new law was passed. The law said that tenements had to have **airshafts** to let light and air into bedrooms.

Although there were windows in rooms next to an airshaft, little air could get through. Airshafts were often blocked because people used the extra space to store things.

This photo of an immigrant family in their tenement at 97 Orchard Street was taken in 1910.

Before 1900, most tenements did not have inside bathrooms. All of the families in the building got their water for cooking, bathing, and washing clothes from one faucet. There was no hot water. When people needed to wash dishes or take a bath, they filled containers with cold water and heated them on the coal-burning stove. They brought a tub into the kitchen and did their washing or bathing there.

Newer apartments had a living room (1), kitchen (2), and two bedrooms (3, 4). Apartments shared a bathroom (5). An airshaft (6) let in light and air. People hung their clean washing on the roof to dry (7).

Life in the Streets

In most parts of New York City, street cleaners picked up garbage. Signs were in English. People spoke English. Food and clothes came from stores. Families and friends visited each other's homes. Children played in parks and on playgrounds.

People usually shopped at **pushcarts.** The Lower East Side was so crowded that people walked in the streets and on the sidewalks.

On the Lower East Side, however, life was like a crowded street fair. Most streets were still paved with rough stones or were not paved at all. This made it hard to keep them clean.

People bought food and clothes from pushcarts. Children ran in and out of the crowds, so carriage- and cart-drivers had to go very slowly. Workers carried huge bundles of clothes to and from workshops and factories.

LANGUAGE

Children learned English more quickly than their parents. They learned at school and on the streets. Parents often learned English at their jobs. They could also take English classes at night school. **Immigrants** wanted to speak and dress like Americans.

People from **Eastern Europe** shopped every day on the streets. Jewish people spoke **Yiddish,** a language that is a mixture of mainly Hebrew and German.

11

Jobs

The Lower East Side was the part of New York City where clothes were made. Workers in **sweatshops** made everything from hats to pants. Many sweatshops were dark, crowded rooms inside **tenements.** Workers often were not allowed to talk to one another. Some sweatshop owners locked the doors to stop workers from leaving early. In 1911, a fire killed many young women making blouses in the Triangle Shirtwaist Factory. They could not get out because the doors had been locked.

PIECE-WORK

Sweatshop workers usually were paid by the piece—for each pocket they made or button they sewed on. This was called **piecework.** A worker just starting out might make as little as $2.50 a week, or about $50 today.

Some women made lace in the living room of their apartments. The women sold their lacework to a **peddler,** who would try and sell it to people on the streets.

A person who had saved a little money might start his or her own business. Peddlers could buy a **pushcart.** Pushcarts carried everything from clothes and furniture to fruits and vegetables. A person with a few hundred dollars could start a candy store or an ice cream parlor. In 1913, the Lower East Side had more than 100 candy stores and ice cream parlors.

Workers often took work home. Everyone in the family helped. This family is making wreaths for a florist. People used the extra money they made to bring family members from the old country to live in the United States.

Clothes

On the streets of the Lower East Side, it was easy to spot **immigrants.** They often wore **traditional** clothes of the country they came from. Women dressed in layers of clothes and covered their heads with shawls or scarves. The men had long beards or mustaches and wore big hats.

These Italian immigrants are wearing clothes similar to those people wore in Italy. Immigrants made their own clothes from lengths of cloth bought in stores or at **pushcarts.**

To blend in, immigrants bought new clothes as soon as they could. The fashion at the time was for women to wear long dresses or a long skirt and a shirt. Their large hats were trimmed with feathers or artificial flowers. Men dressed in long pants, vests, jackets, and hats. Young girls wore dresses that came to their ankles. Young boys wore short pants that came to their knees.

CLOTHES NAMES

American clothes of the early 1900s included the following:
- bowler—man's tall hat with a round top.
- knickerbockers—boys' short pants
- leg-o-mutton sleeves—long sleeves on women's clothes that were puffed at the top
- shirtwaist—blouse that women wore with skirts.

Wealthy Americans took a Saturday afternoon stroll along Broadway in their finest clothes. The man on the right is wearing a suit and top hat. The ladies have on long dresses and large hats. On the left is a policeman.

Ready-to-Wear

Before the 1870s, **tailors** and dressmakers made clothes. People who wanted a new outfit went to a shop and ordered it. By the end of the 1800s, however, inventions such as the sewing machine made it cheaper and faster to make clothing. Hundreds of shirts, dresses, coats, or pants could be cut from one **pattern.** Clothes made in this way were called ready-to-wear because people could buy them and put them on right away.

Immigrants worked many hours each day in **sweatshops** on the Lower East Side. From a larger factory, they received pieces of cloth cut from patterns. Using sewing machines, they made ready-to-wear knee pants for a clothes store.

Because ready-to-wear clothes were made in factories and sweatshops, fewer skilled people were needed. Instead of paying high wages to a tailor, factories hired workers to do **piecework,** or make parts of a piece of clothing. This was good news for the immigrants. They could get work even if they did not have the skills of a tailor or dressmaker.

FACTORY BOSSES

Factory owners often took advantage of "greenhorns"—a negative name for new immigrants. One boss said, "I want no experienced girls. They know the pay to get ... but these greenhorns ... cannot speak English and they don't know where to go and they just come from the old country, and I let them work hard ...for less wages."

Wealthy women shopped for hats, ribbons, and bows in large stores in New York.

Children

On the Lower East Side, children had to work from an early age. Six- and seven-year-olds helped their parents do **piecework.** Girls as young as ten often took care of the younger children while their parents worked. Parents wanted their children to go to school, but they needed the money that the children could earn.

In the 1890s, alley gangs started up on the Lower East Side. Alleys were the narrow walkways behind or between **tenements.** Children played in alleys and some picked the pockets of passersby.

Most children did not play with toys. They found their fun in the streets. They sneaked rides on passing carts. In hot weather, they ran through water spraying from open fire hydrants.

Newsboys and girls sold newspapers on the streets. **Immigrant** families needed even the few pennies this brought in.

In the alleys, children played a game called stickball. They used a board as a baseball bat. If they did not have a baseball, they used a small block of wood as a ball. These wooden "balls" often broke windows or hit people passing by, so stickball players had to be ready to run!

Schools

The Pledge of Allegiance was written in 1892 in honor of Columbus Day. After that, many schools began each day with the "Pledge to the Flag," as it was called then.

In the old country, most boys did not stay in school past the age of ten or twelve. Girls did not go to school at all. Their parents thought they should learn to cook and take care of the family. But New York City law said that boys and girls had to go to school until they were fourteen.

School was not easy for **immigrant** children. Other students, and at times teachers, made fun of greenhorns' clothing and poor English. Every day, students' hands and clothes were checked. If their clothes or fingernails were dirty, or if they fell asleep in class, they were punished.

The teachers did not live in **tenements.** They often did not realize that the children did not have water in their homes, or that they did **piecework** until late at night.

Classrooms were crowded on the Lower East Side. These elementary school children watch their teacher write on the blackboard.

Transportation

Public transportation made it possible for **immigrants** to get away from the Lower East Side. As soon as they could make enough money, they moved to another part of the city.

To get to work, they could take a streetcar. Horses pulled streetcars along metal tracks. It cost five or ten cents for a ride. But drivers could not go very fast. They had to watch carefully for people, animals, and **pushcarts** crossing the tracks.

Before there were streetcars, people rode in carriages. They also used omnibuses, which were wooden cars pulled by horses. People used carriages to carry goods as well as people.

THE SUBWAY

In 1904, the first subway line in New York City opened. It carried riders underground from City Hall to Grand Central Station and on to Times Square. By the 1920s, two more companies had built subway tunnels to carry riders to Brooklyn and other parts of New York City.

By 1870, elevated trains ran on tracks high above the street. People called this kind of train the "el" for short. As they roared along the tracks, els showered dirt and ashes onto passengers inside the cars and people on the street below.

Since Manhattan—where the Lower East Side is located—is an island, there was only so much room to grow. The streets were getting too crowded for streetcars and buses. The city built new types of public transportation. Passenger trains ran through underground tunnels and along elevated tracks. Ferries carried people across the river to Brooklyn, Staten Island, and New Jersey.

Food

Many **immigrants** introduced foods from their countries to the United States. Many of the foods we enjoy today were first eaten on the Lower East Side. Immigrants made dill pickles, hot dogs, bagels, and pretzels. The immigrants also learned to enjoy foods they had never seen before, such as bananas.

A group of young boys wearing knickerbockers buy pretzels from a **peddler.**

Recipe—Latkes

Many of the foods the immigrants made were for holidays they had celebrated in the old country. They served them to their new friends and neighbors. Soon, people from many countries were eating dishes such as corned beef or spaghetti with tomato sauce. Jewish people ate **latkes,** or potato pancakes, during Hanukkah, the Jewish festival of lights.

WARNING: Do not cook anything unless there is an adult to help you. Always ask an adult to help you use the stove, handle hot foods, and use a grater.

YOU WILL NEED
6 potatoes, peeled
2 beaten eggs
1 teaspoon salt
1/4 teaspoon pepper
1 small onion, peeled
2 tablespoons flour
1/4 cup oil

FOLLOW THE STEPS
1. Grate the potatoes and the onion into a large bowl.

2. Add the eggs, salt, pepper, and flour. Stir just until everything is mixed.

3. Heat the oil in a heavy frying pan. When the oil sizzles, drop large spoonfuls of the potato mixture into the pan.
4. Cook until brown on one side. Turn the pancakes over and cook until brown.
5. Place cooked pancakes on paper towels to drain.
6. Serve with applesauce or sour cream.

Hard Times

It was hard to stay clean on the Lower East Side. Washing machines had not been invented yet and many **tenements** had no running water. Ashes from coal stoves piled up in the streets with rotten vegetables and other garbage. With 1,000 people per acre, which is about the size of a running track, the Lower East Side was more crowded than any other place in the world. Diseases such as **tuberculosis** spread quickly and killed many people.

Children whose parents had died had no place to go. They might earn a few pennies a day selling newspapers or shining shoes. Sometimes they slept in alleys and doorways.

It was hard to stay safe, too. Some people took advantage of **immigrants.** Tenement owners did not keep their buildings clean or safe. People sometimes had to pay a **bribe** to get a job or a place to live. Thieves and pickpockets roamed the streets, easily hiding in the crowds. People did not like competing with new immigrants for jobs. Police sometimes did not punish people who robbed or mistreated immigrants.

A PLACE TO SLEEP

Some immigrants had families to stay with when they arrived on the Lower East Side. Others paid to stay in a **boardinghouse.** However, many newcomers were not so lucky. They paid a few cents each night to sleep in a **flophouse.** These buildings had filthy rooms with beds made of cloth stretched on a wooden frame.

In a flophouse, some people slept in beds, others on the floor. They slept in the same clothes they wore to work.

27

Settlement Houses

At first, few people paid attention to the way **immigrants** lived. But by the late 1800s, some people thought it was time for a change. Reporters such as Jacob Riis began to write newspaper articles about life on the Lower East Side. These writers were known as muckrakers, because they brought up things that wealthy people did not want to know about.

This immigrant family was thrown out of their **tenement** on the Lower East Side because they could not pay the rent. The family and their furniture were left on the street. They had little hope of finding a new home quickly.

Nurses leave the Henry Street Settlement House to help poor people living on the Lower East Side.

LILLIAN WALD

Lillian Wald was a nurse who wanted to help immigrants. In 1893, she started the first visiting nurse service in the United States. Nurses went to immigrants' homes to help the sick and to teach people how to stay healthy. They also went to schools to teach children about good health. Later, Lillian Wald started the Henry Street Settlement House. Settlement houses were places immigrants could go for help, to take classes, or to relax.

At the same time, other people started settlement houses. These were places where immigrants could learn how to speak English, stay healthy, or even play an instrument. Nurses from settlement houses went into the tenements, taking care of sick people and teaching people how to stop diseases from spreading.

Lower East Side Now

Today, the Lower East Side is home to artists, poets, restaurants, and shops. The factories and sweatshops are gone, but visitors can still buy all kinds of clothing from crowded shops along Orchard and Hester streets. At the Lower East Side Tenement Museum, people can visit apartments that look the same as they did when the **immigrants** lived there.

Tourists and New Yorkers stroll by an apartment building on the Lower East Side today. Living conditions in the apartments and on the streets are sometimes still crowded and noisy.

Glossary

airshaft narrow space between two apartment buildings

boarder person who lives with a family for a set amount of money

boardinghouse place to live where meals are provided

bribe money a person was forced to pay in order to get or keep a job or apartment

Eastern Europe countries such as Hungary, Russia, Poland, Lithuania, and Yugoslavia

famine time when there is not enough food for everyone

flophouse a place to sleep for very little money

immigrant person who moves from one country to live in another

pattern shaped paper placed on top of a stack of fabric, which is then cut around to make pieces of clothing

peddler person who travels around selling things

piecework work that involves making one small piece of clothing. The worker is paid a certain amount for each piece.

pushcart cart with large wheels that peddlers used to carry items they sold

sweatshop crowded, unsafe place where workers make things and are paid and treated poorly

synagogue place where Jews hold worship services

tailor craftworker who is trained to sew and design clothes

tenement apartment house that is very crowded and dirty

traditional word that describes ways of life that have stayed the same for a long time

tuberculosis disease of the lungs that spreads quickly, causing coughing

Yiddish language spoken by Jews from Eastern Europe that is a mixture of Hebrew, German, and other languages

More Books to Read

An older reader can help you with these books.

Bial, Raymond. *Tenement: Immigrant Life on the Lower East Side.* Boston: Houghton Mifflin, 2002.

Granfield, Linda. *97 Orchard Street: Stories of Tenement Life.* Toronto: Tundra Books, 2001.

Index